T0045220

Old Boat, New Boat

Written by
Rob Waring and **Maurice Jamall**

Before You Read

to clean

money

to fix something

truck

to paint

window

to sell

broken

beach

new boat

engine

old boat

In the story

Tyler   Faye   David   Ryan   Mr. Walsh

"Let's put it here," Mr. Walsh says to his son, Ryan.
Mr. Walsh has an old boat. He does not want it now.
They are putting his old boat on the beach.
Ryan says, "But, Dad, we can't put the boat here!"
Mr. Walsh says, "Ryan, it's okay. Nobody is looking."

Ryan helps his father. They put the old boat on the beach. Ryan sees a man. The man is walking his dog on the beach. "Dad," he says, "Somebody is coming. Come on! Let's go!" Ryan's father says, "Okay. Let's go."

The next morning, some people come to the beach.
One of the boys sees the old boat. His name is Tyler.
"Look at that!" says Tyler. "That's a nice boat!" he says.
Tyler's friend David says, "No, it's not. It's broken. It's no good."
Their friend Faye is looking at the boat, too.

Tyler says, "But we can fix it, and then we can have it!"
David says, "But it's not ours."
"I know. It's not ours," says Tyler. ". . . but nobody wants it. We can fix it, and then it can be *our* boat."
"Tyler, that's a great idea," says Faye.

Then, two men come to the beach. They look at the boat.
"What are you doing?" David asks one man.
"We're taking the boat away," says the man.
David asks, "Whose boat is it?"
"I don't know," says the man. "It's a good boat, but nobody wants it."

"Can we have it?" asks Tyler. "We can fix the boat," he says.

"That's a great idea," says the man.

Tyler asks, "So, can we have it, please?"

The man says, "Yes, I think it's okay."

"Great! Thanks," Tyler says. He's very happy.

"Let's come back and get it on Saturday," says Faye. David says, "My father has a truck. He doesn't work on Saturday. He can help us."

"But the boat has no engine," says David. "And we don't have any money."

"I know!" says Faye. "But we can work and get some money. Then we can buy things for the boat."

"Good thinking!" says David.

The next day they work to get some money.
Faye sells some hot dogs at the beach. Tyler plays music in the town. And David cleans windows. They get a lot of money.
They can buy many things for the boat.

On Saturday, they take the boat to David's house.
David's father, Mr. Robinson helps them. He gives
them an engine for the boat.
Tyler and Mr. Robinson fix the boat.
Faye and David paint it. It is looking good now.
But Ryan is watching them.

Tyler says, "This old boat looks great now!"
"This *new* boat looks great, Tyler," says Faye.
Everybody smiles. They are very happy to have a boat.
"Let's take the boat to the beach," says David. "And let's go out in it."
Mr. Robinson takes the boat to the beach.

On the beach Ryan sees the boat.

"Wow, my boat looks great now," he thinks. He wants it back.

He says, "That's my boat! I want it back."

"No, Ryan," says Faye. "It's *our* boat."

Ryan says, "Give it back to me! It's mine."

"Do you really want your *old* boat, Ryan?" asks Tyler.

Ryan says, "Yes I do. Give me back my boat."

"Okay," says Tyler. "You can have it."
Tyler takes some things out of the boat. "But these are ours.
You can't have them," he says.
They start taking things off the boat.
"Stop!" says Ryan. "That's my boat! Those things are mine!"
Faye says, "And this is our engine. Now give us money for the
paint."
David says, "And give us money for fixing it."

The man comes back to the beach. He hears them talking.
"Is this your boat?" the man asks Ryan.
Ryan says, "Yes, it's mine."
"Oh, you put this boat on the beach. Then give me $200,"
says the man. "You can't put this on the beach."
Ryan is worried. "$200?" he thinks.
"Umm . . . no," he says now. "It's not my boat. It's theirs."

Ryan goes away. Tyler looks at the man. They smile.
"Thanks," says Tyler.
"You have a great new boat now," says the man.
David says, "Ryan's *old* boat. But our *new* boat!"